PREAMBLE

Two or three generations ago it was ac_____ ___ ___ __ _ ____
lim Mentality'[1] as if it were reasonable to tidily summarise how
hundreds of millions of human beings thought and acted despite
their global dispersion, cultural diversity and vast numbers.

Thankfully, such careless generalising is no longer welcomed
when talking of Muslims (or for that matter any ethnic, geo-
graphic, etc. group of people). Some recognition is now given to
the vast extent of Islamic cultural, geographical and historical diversity.

Nonetheless, some generalisations about Islam can be attempted –
not concerning traits or personalities, but concerning the events
and ideas that over history have unified Muslims. To illustrate
with the obvious: Muslims have always revered both Mohammed
and the Qur'an. They have always seen their faith as giving practical, concrete ways to live in a Godly way. These are centred in
the 'Five Pillars' (profession of faith, ritual prayer, fasting, pil-
grimage to Mecca, regular giving of *zakat* alms). Such concrete
measures are not always followed – but they are invariably seen as
valid, correct ways of pleasing God.

This brief paper will give a broad overview (with some illustrative
details) of the events and ideas that have unified in the past, and
continue to unify in the present, Muslims across the globe.

A GENERAL INTRODUCTION TO ISLAM

Introduction

It seems that the habit of generalising about how large groups of
people behave is at least as old as Biblical times, if we can take
the comment St Paul made to Titus at face value.[2] It is no longer
socially acceptable to suggest that groups categorised by faith,
ethnicity, geography, interests, etc. can be meaningfully described
en masse – but we continue, nonetheless, to organise our knowledge by categorising the things we encounter and then make our
predictions on the characteristics each category manifests. We
continue, in other words, to rely on generalisations. Such catego-
rising-theorising-and-prediction is, after all, central to the scien-
tific method by which we make sense of the world. Moreover, like all habits[3], using generalisations seems to get results
quickly with little apparent effort or thought.

And it seems this paper will continue the habit of generalising: do
I not, after all, hope to give some sort of over-arching ideas concerning Islam and, by extrapolation, more than 1,000,000,000 human beings across the globe?

There are, however, a couple of 'health warnings' at the start of
this generalised introduction to Islam. The first concerns all generalisations.

While they may well ease the handling of large pieces of knowledge ('Bangladesh is poor') which can result in effective
responses ('so resources should be diverted to Bangladesh'), they
cannot grapple with complexity ('what, precisely, does poverty
mean?') nor can there be an extrapolation from a generalisation to
an individualised assessment ('this person is Bangladeshi therefore she/he is poor').

Secondly, and of more immediate relevance, is the fact that this paper will not, in fact, deal primarily with either Islam or Muslims. Instead, it will look at the prevailing historical and ideological climate that surrounds Muslims. To use an analogy, rather than commenting on what types of clothing Scottish people wear, I will concern myself with the Scottish climate and the implications this might have regarding clothing. Because all who live in Scotland experience the same climate, there may well be some simil- arities in apparel: because every human being varies significantly, there will also be observable variations. By extension, because there are prevailing influences that significantly impact on all Muslims across the world, there may well be similarities that emerge (alongside individualised variations). These prevailing influences are centred on two main themes: what has happened to Muslims (Islamic history) and what Muslims have thought about their rela- tionship with God (Islamic theology and mysticism). It is these themes that will be explored throughout this paper.

THE HISTORICAL BACKGROUND OF MODERN ISLAM

'If you know your history, then you would know where you are coming from' is how Bob Marley (in his 'Buffalo Soldier') suggested that who we are is informed by our past experiences. The collective Islamic memory about history could be divided into five (very) broad historical periods. The first of these is the time of establishment-and-consolidation; the second, a time of Absolutism;[4] the third, of Commonwealth; the fourth, of absolutism (without a capital letter); and finally, a time of reaction (to the European colonial invasions). This final period continues to this day – unless it is believed that a sixth period consisting of Islamic resurgence is underway.

The Establishment, Expansion and Consolidation of Islam

Perhaps the best analogy to understand the Arabian Peninsula that Mohammed was born into in 570 CE is Mongolia throughout the 1970s and 1980s: a vast, remote and underpopulated area surrounded by superpowers. To the west was the Byzantine Empire which had grown out of the earlier Roman Empire. Under Constantine, Christianity had become the state religion in 313 CE and the capital was shifted eastwards from Rome to Constantinople (modern-day Istanbul). This eastern wing would become a separate, sole-surviving entity after the sacking of Rome in 408 CE. Although Christianity was the state religion of Byzantium, the centre's Hellenistic strain often clashed with local forms of faith. There were other theological divisions within the Empire as well (although it may be more correct to suggest that an existing urban/rural divide found its expression in theological terms). Byzantium was also weakened in the time before Mohammed's birth by recurrent attacks of the plague, earthquakes, and ongoing war with the Sassanians. They were the other seventh-century regional superpower. Situated to the east of the Arabian Peninsula, the Sassanians also began the seventh century ostensibly powerful but actually weakened by internal disputes. These primarily centred on local interests trying to retain a measure of power against central control which claimed for itself both dynastic and divine rights to govern.

Mohammed was born in Mecca, which is situated in the isolated and mountainous zone of the Arabian Peninsula between the deserts of the interior and the Red Sea. By the seventh century CE it was on the lucrative trade route between Yemen and the Mediterranean, between the two above-mentioned superpowers. He was, then, born into an apparently marginalised area quirkily situated in between two major powers – but actually on a major pathway in between two rapidly declining empires.

This brief article will not examine the life of Mohammed itself – that subject would fittingly form a separate study – but it can be briefly noted that his twenty-three years of preaching, teaching and leading were divided into two contrasting periods of around a decade each. The first began around 610 CE, with the first Revelation.[5] Over the next decade Mohammed would overcome uncertainty, gain reassurance from those closest to him, and gather around 150 close disciples. The number was too large to be easily ignored, particularly since some (including Mohammed himself) had a measure of protective family/tribal connections. 150 was, however, far too few to effectively govern society or even feel secure. The second, decade-long, period of Mohammed's work dates from the 'flight' from Mecca to Medina, a shift that was so influential that the Islamic calendar begins from this time. In Medina, Mohammed had an ever-increasing leadership role, the number of Believers grew quickly, and the expansion of Islam began.

Until Mohammed died in 12/632, he and the new Believers went on more than a dozen military expeditions. The first was essentially a raid[6] quickly followed by the first important encounter – the Battle of Badr. While not all battles would be as successful as Badr, success and expansion were very definitely the pattern throughout the remainder of Mohammed's life – and beyond it.

Mohammed's leadership was pivotal in this success.[7] He used others' expertise when appropriate[8] and made sense out of occasions that could have been interpreted as setbacks.[9] In addition to Mohammed's military and management skills was the ever-widening acceptance that his message – the Qur'an – was a message for all peoples in all times. It was this legacy of successful and theologically significant leadership that was inherited, on Mohammed's death, by the four Caliphs who then would rule from Medina.[10]

Ali,[11] the last of these four, died in 40/661. Islam had, by then, already spread across the Arabian peninsula: north into what is now Syria and Iraq, west as far as the Nile and east as far as central Persia (now Iran) establishing cities such as Basra as it went.

The Time of Absolutism

Expansion did not stop after these four 'Rightly Guided' caliphs were supplanted by the Umayyad Caliphate, but at some point there was a change of focus towards Absolutism. During the ninety years of Umayyad rule, the Islamic regions continued to expand (but not in Mongol-style destroy-and-depart incursions) and consolidate. This was done by (for example) making Arabic the official language and by the establishment of governing departments. Conversions to Islam continued, giving further consolidation, although the details of how this came about are not easy to discover at this historical distance. For Muslims, the explanation is simply that people increasingly recognised the truth. Certainly, a foundational change of heart did prompt unknown numbers to convert, perhaps aided by the fact that many Christians of the time may well have seen Islam less as a new religion than a new and attractive sect of their own, deeply-divided, faith. It is also certain that military coercion was not the primary motivation, despite this being an often cited reason in European writings of an earlier age.

The change of focus to Absolutism entailed a change whereby Islam became accepted as being more than one person's message in an isolated region to being seen as a Message for all, at all times. The Caliphate was established as a form of governance whose rule had both temporal and spiritual authority. This change neither happened overnight, nor at the precise point of regime change (from Ali to the Umayyads, or the Umayyads to the Abbasids). Indeed, questions about how much freedom a leader had to interpret the Qur'an and *hadith* to govern in new circumstances would emerge as a major issue as late as the reign of (eighth Abbasid Caliph) Al-Mu'tasim in the third/ninth century.[12] Expansion, too, continued; by the time the Abbasid Caliphate had established itself, the *Dar al-Islam* (i.e. the area under Islamic Rule) incorporated the Sind (in current Southern Pakistan), North Africa, Spain and Transoxiana (north-eastern Afghanistan).

The Damascus-based Umayyad Caliphate lasted from 41/661–132/750. The following Abbasid Caliphate which lasted from 132/750 to the early fourth/ninth century was centred in Iraq around a purpose-built capital city – Baghdad. Construction was begun in 145/762 under (second Caliph) al-Mansur after he had carefully chosen a site that was central and accessible. The Abbasid Caliphate perhaps reached its height under the fifth Caliph, Harun al Rashid, who ruled from 170/786 – 193/809. Islam was, by this stage, centre stage in global terms. It had a well-governed Empire, centres of learning[13] and relative security. Far from occupying a neglected corner of a deserted region, Islam was now at the centre and it was Europe that appeared peripheral.

The Time of Commonwealth

After Harun al-Rashid, the Abbasid Caliphate had another almost four-and-a-half centuries to run, although for the final half (at least) of this the Caliphate was essentially devoid of power outside central Iraq (and sometimes barely outside Baghdad). Baghdad itself was destroyed by the Mongols in 656/1258 but from the third/ninth century onward, there was no longer a single, centralised Islamic government that could claim to rule all Muslims. Instead a commonwealth of states emerged that acted in some ways together, and had some shared allegiance (however slight) to a central government. The satellite states tended to last three generations, beginning with a charismatic leader who rallied people by referring to the injustices and corruptions of a faraway, central government. Next, there was a successor (usually a son) who stabilised the movement but who lacked the skills to either expand the founder's vision, or completely institutionalise a new way of governing. Finally, the third generation squandered the fledgling state, which then began to collapse (although this might take several decades to come about). This extremely truncated summary cannot, of course, give much idea regarding the complexities of dynasties as diverse as the Fatimids,[14] the Buyids,[15] the Seljuqs,[16] etc. It can, however, be noted that these smaller states were not necessarily lesser states since some of the greatest achievements of Islam whether measured artistically, militarily, architecturally, etc. occurred within this commonwealth of states.

The Time of absolutism

It would not seem likely, on the face of it, that there would be any age, or time, at all for Islam following the Mongols. They decimated all of central Asia, reducing entire cities. Baghdad was only one of the cities that, essentially, ceased to exist. That Islam itself did not end at this point could be seen as proof that power had already been decentralised and regional powers arisen – except that many of these regional cities were also decimated. Perhaps, however, such decentralisation had not only occurred, it had gone far beyond the political sharing-out of power to a diffusion of Islam from a centre into disparate peripheries.[17] While the Mongols could continue, generation after generation, to sometimes literally pile up the skulls from slaughtered cities, it was perhaps the body rather than the soul of Islam they were destroying.[18] It could even be argued that the Mongols contributed to the revitalisation of Islam by ridding it of accretions and distractions. It is, at least, evident that once the Mongol invasions had receded, a viable form of governance that was part-way between the decentralised, short-lived dynasties and the over-arching Absolutism of the Umayyads and the Abbasids, quickly arose. This governance took the form of two long-term, large-scale Empires, the Ottomans and the Mughals.[19]

The Mughals ruled over India for almost five centuries. The first Muslims to enter the subcontinent in force were in fact the Ghaznavids who made almost twenty raids into Northern India between 340/1000 and 370/1030. Next were the Ghurids who were also essentially raiders, but made a base in Delhi, rather than returning *en masse* to Central Asia (Ghazni being south of modern Kabul). Humayun was the first Mughal leader, but the dynasty as a whole really began with his successor, Akbar, who began his rule in 963/1556 and became the first person to unite India since

Asoka, nearly two thousand years earlier. To say the Mughals ruled over an enormous Islamic Empire is true, although Akbar himself was almost syncretistic in his beliefs and practices of faith. Later rulers, in particular Aurangzeb, (who ruled from 1068/1658 to 1118/1707) were far more strict in their observances of Islam but the Mughals were, nonetheless, Islamic rulers over a huge part of the globe until the British encroachment began in 1765 CE.

The Ottomans were the other 'absolutist' dynasty that arose in the wake of Mongol decimation. As well as having intrinsic importance as rulers over such a vast, diverse and long-lasting Islamic empire, the Ottomans were also important because many of the working arrangements between Europe (whose aspirations to empire began to impinge on the Middle East from 1798 CE onwards) and the *Dar al-Islam* (the areas where the Islamic rule was established) were first worked out within the Ottoman Empire. *Tanzimat* Reforms, for example, were promulgated partly to ease trade between the two 'superpowers' who had differing legal codes[20] but a shared imperative to trade due to their own citizens' demands and desires. A Mixed Court system, established in 1875 CE, widened Europeans' legal rights, and a year later *Majalla* changes led to Muslims and non-Muslims being equally treated in Ottoman criminal law. European colonialism,[21] at least in this overt form, would end its working relationship with the Ottoman Empire when the Ottoman Empire itself ended, a casualty of the First World War, in 1917 CE.

The Reaction to Invasion

The above summary of Islamic history, convoluted though it may appear, cannot give more than a hint of the complexity entailed in 1500 years of widely-dispersed, hugely differing, regimes. It would be a mistake to assume any particular, individual Muslim has even this summarised sense of Islamic history – but what can be assumed with some certainty is that she/he knows that Islam did once rule vast tracts of the earth effectively and continuously.[22] Any particular Muslim is likely to know core details about the life of Mohammed and the times of the four 'Rightly Guided' Caliphs, something about important Abbasid Caliphs such as Harun al-Rashid, and the Islamic history of their own particular region – and (more importantly) be confident that, given time and study, encouraging details of how well Islam once ruled the better part of the world are ready to be discovered.

Islamic history has, in other words, had long periods when Muslims' relationships with non-Muslim neighbours were conducted from a position of power and overall superiority. They were more than self-reliant; other powers came more as supplicants than colonisers. The end of the Ottoman Empire meant the end of the last Islamic 'superpower'. Muslim countries may still have power, of course, but for at least a century the *Dar al-Islam* has existed in a reactive state to European/Western political supremacy and invasions (few, perhaps, in Europe view their countries' colonial expansions as invasions: equally few, perhaps, of those African and Asian countries who were once under European rule see it as anything else). The most highly-publicised reaction to the relegation of Islam in the global order is, of course, the actions of so-called 'fundamentalists' (the term 'extremists' is, arguably, more apt since many Muslims would argue that attributes such as compassion and peacefulness are more fundamental to

Islam than armed struggle). But there is a far more widespread, albeit less headline-grabbing, dismay at Islam's eroded position at the expense of Europe and America over the past two centuries. This is partly because of the inherent injustice involved, and also (perhaps) partly because of the difficulty in understanding how such an unjust situation could have come about – as we shall now see.

CREATOR AND CREATION: THEOLOGY AND MYSTICISM

If one half of the climate surrounding Muslims in the world today involves 'what we have done and had done to us' (i.e. history and how it is interpreted), the other half involves 'who we are as created beings and how we relate to our Creator' (i.e. theology and mysticism). It is this second aspect that will now be looked at.

How Can We Comprehend God's Will for Our Lives? The Realm of the *Shari'ah*

One crucial element in the examination of how we, as created beings, should relate to our Creator will only be perfunctorily dealt with in this paper (since it has already been dealt with more fully in a separate publication) – the *Shari'ah*. *Shari'ah* is usually translated as 'Islamic law', although this is both an overstatement, and an understatement. It is an overstatement since the *Shari'ah*[23] has never yet provided a complete legal system in Islamic society but has always been supplemented by mechanisms such as the *qanun* laws operated by the Ottomans during their rule. It is also an understatement because the *Shari'ah* has an importance that goes far beyond its legal role alone. Calls to re-introduce the *Shari'ah* have become a central demand in the reclaiming of identity that Muslims across the world are now undertaking.

Moreover, the *Shari'ah* was never really envisaged as merely a set of laws, but as an all-encompassing code which would govern every aspect of everyone's life in order that they might be found righteous before God. Rather than a mechanism that combined moral values with pragmatic measures to maximise societal peace and cohesion (as European legal codes tend to be), the *Shari'ah* aims to give peace on earth and a hope for eternity.

One ramification of having a code that sees no distinction between this- and other-worldly laws is that things that happen in this world are seen to have other-worldly implications. Thus, for example, it becomes hard to see the loss of Empire as simply the result of political changes, or chance discoveries, or the vagaries of some powers reaching the zenith of their strength at the precise time when an advantage could be more-or-less fixed into place.[24] Loss of empire must prompt a religious examination.

Another way of saying this is that Islam is, in some aspects, a very practical faith. It is neither an entirely 'other-worldly' nor a 'here-and-now' faith. Instead, Islam suggests that God's favour is likely to result in both this, and next, world benefits ('suggests' rather than proves, since no-one can presume to know what God actually will do). This means any set-back is theologically difficult to explain.[25] Losing an empire to another power is like 'being promised the earth then made to eat dirt' (in the words of the poet Artnoy Dosh).

How Can We Apprehend God's Will For Our Lives? The Realm of Sufism

Islamic mysticism is known by the term 'Sufism' – but this simple statement hides several levels of complexity. For example, although the historical development of Sufism can be traced,[26] the central experience of being a Sufi remains ambiguously ephemeral and indefinable.[27] Historically, Sufis were one of the main groups who contested for leadership after Mohammed's death. Pious individuals (such as Hasan al-Basri[28]), who reacted to scholars' obtuseness and rulers' impiety[29] with asceticism and single-minded devotion to God, gave way in time to organised Sufi 'schools' (*tariqa*[30]). Sociologically, it has been said that Sufism appeals to three specific groups[31] but it could be more generally suggested

15

that it attracts because it fulfils two important social functions. Firstly, it centralises one aspect of Islamic faith (love, of God, by God, and between people[32]) and thus provides a rationale for not following the *Shari'ah* in all its details while remaining within the commonly accepted boundaries of Islam.

Secondly, it could be argued that Sufism postulates an achievable way of being righteous before God on the Day of Judgement. The reality of this event is a major Qur'anic theme, yet what criteria will be used for judgement is far from clear. Sufism promotes the complete reliance on a spiritual guide as a necessity for success on that Day. Because this verges on blasphemous ideas of intercession, such thoughts are often blurred by symbolic writing. Perhaps this, along with the sheer impossibility of describing mystical experiences, explains why so many of the aphorisms Sufis themselves have described Sufism by are more reminiscent of Buddhist koans (with their sudden, unexpected denouement[33]) or Hindu ambiguity[34] than academic tomes or legalistic arguments.[35]

Rather than relying on intellectual knowledge then, Sufism aims to bring people closer to God by exploring states and experiences. It parallels intellectual, theological knowledge with its own experiential knowledge – but it must be noted that Sufism is no more a monolithic entity than Islamic legal structures are (with their four major, and many more minor, 'schools'). Sufi 'schools' vary in areas such as the degree of centralised organisation, or the closeness of saint and devotee.[36]

Sufism thus remains 'not easy to sum up or define'[37] since it concerns the apprehension rather than the comprehension of God.[38] While shared sensations and exploration of states can give a sense of certainty (albeit one that cannot be coherently discussed[39]) and solidarity amongst the explorers, it is far from settled whether these searchers are within the bounds of the *Shari'ah*, in contravention of it and thus illegal, or an elect[40] that cannot be judged by normal standards ('Let the lover be'[41]). While the *Shari'ah* and Sufism tend to avoid potentially divisive challenges to each other's authority, some still question whether Sufism is a part of, or apart from, Islam.

CONCLUSION

It is a central belief of Christianity that all human beings are created as unique beings: to describe vast numbers of unknown people with blanket generalisations would therefore seem to be incompatible with core Christian beliefs (Paul's comments to Titus regarding Cretans notwithstanding). The Christian faith would therefore seem to concur with our wariness of drawing any wide-ranging conclusions about hundreds of millions of people based on cursory knowledge of a few dozen, or even hundreds/thousands of them.

Part of the fascination, however, of Islam is the very existence of Islamic unity – not uniformity – despite huge disparities of culture, language, history etc. across the Muslim world. Muslims do appear to share more than the rituals and core texts of faith. This does not, of course, imply that all Muslims know even the cursory history of the Caliphate outlined above, much less that they sit around and discuss vexed questions such as whether Harun al-Rashid really was the greatest Abbasid Caliph, or whether Ibn Arabi's monism really ought to have been challenged. Clearly, few people anywhere consider such issues – but part of the unity of Muslims concerns the shared knowledge that there once was a leadership structure that was long-lived, widespread, and effective (and if they wished to study more, they would learn of figures such as Harun al-Rashid). Moreover, there were Muslim thinkers willing and able to grapple with the most complex and potentially divisive thoughts about what we could know about the unknowable (hence an interest in Ibn Arabi).

This brief paper has not really looked at the unity of Islam (that can be inferred from the solidarity Muslims across the world have with Muslims who face suffering in any single part of it) but it has tried to suggest the underlying influences of history and ideas that help to foster such unity. Not knowing the minutiae of historical detail does not, *per se*, mean someone is immune to the effects of history. For example, those born in the UK are likely to enjoy a high standard of living because of former centuries of imperial power (an expectation of success in international sporting events may also form part of the legacy left by long-term, widespread, domination).

The Islamic world also had long periods of widespread domination, but these have now been superseded by several centuries of subjugation. During the centuries of Islamic dominance (either as a centralised Caliphate or devolved powers with capitals in Cairo, Delhi, Lahore, etc.) Islamic artists, theologians, mystics and jurists all explored what it meant to be a created being under a Creative God as extensively as human history has ever undertaken. This is the legacy Muslims world-wide know they have been left. The knowledge that it is, now, a lapsed legacy left to a Muslim world that is subjugated and distorted by too little or too much money is a knowledge not all Muslims are comfortable about seeing as permanent.

Endnotes

[1] Indeed, a book by L. Levonian published in 1928 was simply called 'Moslem Mentality'.

[2] Paul affirms in Titus 1:12-13 that 'Cretans are always liars, evil brutes, lazy gluttons'; (it is beyond the scope of this paper to consider the vexed question of whether Revelation is considered to be a fax-like transmission of God's perspective which thus arrives without distortions, or alternatively Divine guidance filtered through a flawed human transmitter).

[3] 'Habits are the flywheel of society' is how William James put it; (see W. James, 'The Principles of Psychology', Vol. 1, p. 121).

[4] The terminology is taken from Hodgson (being part of the title of a chapter in Book 2 of Volume 1 of 'The Venture of Islam', Chicago, The University of Chicago Press, 1974).

[5] Surah al ʿAlaq (96) which begins 'Proclaim in the name of thy Lord and Cherisher who created – Created man out of a (mere) clot of congealed blood ...'.

[6] In 2/624 (i.e. year 2 of the Islamic calendar, or 2AH, and 624 of the Christian calendar, or 624CE). It took place at Nakhlah, near Mecca, during Rajab (this was one of the Sacred months which prompted the provision of Surah al-Baqara [2:216-217]).

[7] Muslims could, of course, say that the continuing success of Islam was simply because God was protecting and promoting Islam as the true religion.

[8] At the Battle of the Trench in 5/627, Mohammed appropriated the experience of Salman, a freed slave, who had previously fought as a mercenary in Iran and seen the tactic work effectively.

[9] The Treaty of Hudaybiyah could have appeared at the time to be a victory to the Meccans opposing Mohammed: the fact that the chapter of the Qur'an alluding to it is called Surah al-Fat'h (Victory) reflects how Mohammed was able to turn the occasion to the Muslims' advantage.

[10] Known collectively as the 'Rightly Guided' Caliphs.

[11] Ali would later be seen by one faction of the Muslims – the Shi'ites – as belonging to the lineage from which all paramount Muslim leaders should be drawn.

[12] He reigned from 218/833 – 226/842. The argument about how much power a caliph could legitimately claim appeared as a theological question concerning the created-ness of the Qur'an. To assert that it had been created in time was to suggest that it could be adapted in time, to meet time's changing circumstances. To assert that it was uncreated and co-eternal with God was to say that no human being, however powerful or learned, had the right to alter any of its teachings. Politically, the controversy focused on whether a caliph had the right to claim religious sanction when acting beyond Qur'anic guidance. The argument coincided with the burgeoning power of the Turkic soldiers who had increasingly been used in the Muslim armies.

[13] The Bayt al-Hikmah, part university, part library, and part translation-services (ancient Greek writings amongst those studied), was established in Baghdad in 215/830 under the reign of al-Ma'mun, the seventh Caliph. Papermaking had been learned from Chinese prisoners, captured after the Battle of Talas River, in 751 CE.

[14] Lasting from 297/909 – 567/1171, this arose from a Shi'i sect from North Africa to rule over present-day Algeria, Tunisia, Sicily, Egypt, and Syria. It was under them that the oldest existing university (*Al Alzhar*) was established (in 970 CE, in Cairo).

[15] Centred in Rayy, their dynasty lasted from 320/932 – 454/1062.

[16] This Turkic regime is dated from 431/1040 – 485/1092. Turkic peoples (i.e. those who originated from Turkistan, or – roughly speaking – the region north of Afghanistan) had been part of the Islamic world since they were employed as soldiers in as early as al-Mu'tasim's caliphate (218/833 – 226/842).

[17] This is the view of Bulliet, who expounds the idea in his book 'Islam, the View from the Edge'.

[18] Again, Muslims may well argue that Islam survived simply because it is the true faith and was therefore protected by God – talk of cities, centres, peripheries, or personalities merely signposts how this protection occurred.

[19] And, arguably, the Saffavids and Andalusian rulers too. Andalusia/Spain had been Islamic since late Umayyad times (it was in fact established by the sole survivor of the Umayyad dynasty who escaped the bloody transfer of power to the Abbasids). Spain escaped the Mongol depredations and Islamic rule remained with fluctuating alliances and boundaries until Christianity re-asserted itself in the 15th century CE. Iran also had long-term stability which never resulted in a pan-Islamic empire but did unite a wide region under unified governance in the post-Mongol period. The Saffavids came to power in 1502 CE. They were (probably) originally Kurdish Sunnis, but the dynasty they established over Persia/Iran was Shi'ite, which meant they claimed theological credentials for their leadership alongside those of lineage. The Saffavids provided relatively stable governance for almost two-and-a-half centuries across the region.

[20] These were presaged by the promulgation of a Commercial Code in 1266/1850 which was designed to ease trade; eight years later there was a wholesale adoption of the French penal code. There were tensions within the Ottoman legal system between the Shari'ah and the use of *qanun* (roughly equivalent to case law) around this time as well.

[21] Albeit colonialism sometimes presented as altruism, leading to Muhammed Abduh's poignant epithet, 'Do not attempt to do us any more good. Your good has done us too much harm already', (quoted in Gerald Butt's 'A Rock and a Hard Place', p. 31).

[22] Spain remains the only large area of land that has 'returned' from becoming Islamic.

[23] Which consists of core rulings from the Qur'an and *hadith* as well as mechanisms (known as *qiyas* – analogy, and *ijma* – consensus) by which new rulings can be generated.

21

[24] Abbasid strength, for example, peaked before developments in travel and communication allowed them to extend and concretise their governance across increasingly vast areas.

[25] Technically speaking, it could be suggested that Islam lacks a theodicy, i.e. a theology that can explain suffering. Sociologically, this could explain why the Shi'ite festival of Mohorrum is so widely celebrated despite the fact that Shi'ites only make up a tenth of the global Muslim population (Mohorrum commemorates the death of Husayn in Karbala in 61/680: Husayn was Ali's son and Ali was both the final 'Rightly Guided' Caliph and Mohammed's son-in-law. Because Mohammed did not have any surviving sons of his own, Shi'ites believe that leadership of Muslims should follow the lineage of Ali). It has been noted that although Shi'ites in Bangladesh 'comprise less than one per cent of the population ... over ninety per cent of the Muharram participants and onlookers are Sunni'. (See M. Dunham, 'Jarigan Muslim Epic Songs of Bangladesh', Dhaka, 1997, 6.)

[26] As, for example Trimingham does in his 'The Sufi Orders in Islam', Oxford, 1971.

[27] Indeed 'truth without form' was Ibn al-Jalla's definition of Sufism while other accounts identify Sufism as the 'esoteric' or inward (*bātin*) aspect of Islam which is to be distinguished from 'exoteric' (*zāhir*) (See [tr.] Nicholson, 'Kashf al Mahjub',) 37, 36-41 has several more definitions; and T. Burckhardt, 'An Introduction to Sufi Doctrine', Lahore, 1963, 3.)

[28] Hasan al-Basri (643 CE – 728 CE) was one of the earliest Sufis, known as much for his asceticism as his inspired teachings. (See M. Smith, 'The Way of the Mystics', London, 1976, 174–175.)

[29] Ewing comments that general disenchantment at Islamic governments' movement away from the *Shari'ah* led Shi'ites to focus their hopes on a 'Hidden Imam' while Sunnis turned to 'preserving' saints who maintained global order and localised saints who could be consulted at times of need. Subhan suggests that early

believers withdrew in disgust from the 'tyrannical and impious role of the 'Umayyad *khalifas'* and dates the later rise in speculative thoughts to Ma'mun's leadership (198/813 – 218/833). (See K. Ewing, 'The Pir or Sufi Saint in Pakistani Islam', unpublished PhD thesis, University of Chicago, 1980, 27; J. Subhan, 'Sufism Its Saints and Shrines', Lucknow, 1938, 10.)

[30] Each *tariqa* was marked by its own spiritual exercises, although more generally there was a shared format whereby seven stages had to be consecutively negotiated. These were repentance, fear of God, renunciation, poverty, patience (or endurance), surrender to (or trust in) God, and contentment ('whatever befalls the traveller is a blessing for him'). Complete devotion to one's spiritual guide was also generally required. (See C. Rice, 'The Persian Sufis', London, 1969, 32, 35, 39-54.)

[31] The first is the dispossessed, wanting to escape from their difficult situation; the second is the urban middle class anxious to reconnect to their roots; the third is those seeking to influence the ruling powers. (See M. Gilsenan, 'Recognising Islam', New York, 1982, 244–245.)

[32] 'The worship of God based on love' is one description of Sufism (see Rice, *op. cit.*, 34).

[33] Often involving overturned tables or similarly abrupt actions that startle an acolyte into enlightenment.

[34] Such as the Hindu description of God as *neti neti* (neither this thing nor that thing; nothing, in other words, that the mind can conceive of). This consistency with Hindu ideas facilitated the acceptance of Islam in the Indian subcontinent.

[35] This mention of other faiths should not obscure the insistence of most Muslim writers in tracing Sufism to Mohammed rather that extraneous sources such as Greek, Christian, Hindu or Buddhist. (See, for example, M. Rahmān, 'Mārephāter Gaupan Rahasýa', Dhaka: Chowdury and Sons, nd, 64-65.)

[36] One writer splits formal Sufism into the two 'complexes' of Sufi

sectarianism and popular Islam. He then divides popular Islam into the *sharif* complex (which honours Mohammed's family) and the *walī* complex (which essentially maximises the importance of emulating Mohammed). Devotees in the *walī* complex gather rather than are ranked around the saint, and relationships rather than exercises are the key to spiritual growth. (See R. Reeves, 'The Sufi Complex at Tanta, Egypt: An Ethnographic Approach to Popular Islam', an unpublished PhD thesis, Kentucky, 1981, 405-406).

[37] See Rice, *op. cit.*, 9.

[38] Shabistari (died circa 720/1320) suggested that Sufism 'is a way beyond the reason by which a man is able to know the secret of reality' while Bulliet writes that 'in very simple terms, Sufis seek the psychological experience of union with or vision of God through a graded series of ritual and meditative exercises, including asceticism and worldly denial'. (See G. Rasool, 'Chisti-Nizami Sufi Order of Bengal', Delhi, 1990, 3; and R. Bulliet, 'Islam, The View from the Edge', New York, 1995, 90.)

[39] Attar writes 'in the School of the Secret you will see thousands of men with intellectual knowledge, their lips parted in silence. What is intellectual knowledge here? It stops on the threshold of the door like a blind child'; while Rumi suggests 'you don't understand until you are what you're trying to understand' . (See [tr.] C. Nott, 'Conference of the Birds' by Farid ud-din Attar, London, 1985, 116; C. Barks and I. Khan, 'The Hand of Poetry', New York, 1993, 89.)

[40] Those few whose 'every mouthful and saying is lawful' (in Rumi's words) and who follow a purer form of faith which they then present in a simplified form to the many. (See [tr.] R. Nicholson, 'The Mathnavi of Jalalu'Uddin Rumi', Delhi, 1992, [Vols I and II], 89.

[41] The line is from a quatrain of Jalal Uddin Rumi's:

> 'Let the lover be disgraceful, crazy,
> absentminded. Someone sober
> will worry about events going badly.
> Let the lover be.'

(See J. Moyne and C. Barks, 'Unseen Rain', np, 1986, 7)

Published by:
©Rutherford House
17 Claremont Park
Edinburgh EH6 7PJ
Tel: 0131 554 1206
Fax:
Email: info
IS

09460   68038